I loved reading *Able Soul*–
Written and constructed in short chapters i̶ ̶ ̶ ̶ ̶ ̶ ̶ /
work as a daily devotional, or an absorbing one sitting read from cover to cover, or as an occasional "fire-side" book that one can come back to again and again. Whichever way, the reader will laugh, cry, pray, reflect, and learn as Lucy Goncalves draws insightful analogies from the challenges and triumphs of her own life as someone with cerebral palsy. It is a strikingly honest account that is sometimes lighthearted, and other times raw and disturbing. But through it all one will learn profound lessons of amazing grace, God's love, personal accountability, courage, and keys to overcoming set-backs to get the very best out of life. Lucy is a much loved member of our church.

—Graham Fletcher, Pastor of C3 Church Vancouver
Author and Itinerant Minister

Modern society flaunts success based on physical ability and social status; very clearly implying that the value of each life is determined by outward image, physical performance and social achievement.

Able Soul is a wake-up call to all of us.

Today's society has lost its soul, and it has lost its way. We may be "physically able", but with suicide, bullying, self-harm, violence, and depression at an all-time high, we all need an "able soul", like Lucy.

Thank you to Lucy for this book that opens our mind and our heart to a different way of thinking and living. Society needs this gift, and Lucy you are showing us the way to an Able Soul.

—Carrie Williams, Former Executive Director
Signal Hill Life Education Society

Able Soul

Empowering God's Spirit Within

Able Soul

Empowering God's Spirit Within

Lucy Goncalves

Published by Able Soul Wheel Press
Vancouver, Canada

ISBN 978-1-9990326-1-6 (paperback)
ISBN 978-1-9990326-0-9 (ebook)

Interior design by Sun Editing & Book Design
Cover design by Candesign
Back cover photo by Shaun Huberts

Printed in Canada

---

http://ablesoul.ca
https://www.facebook.com/ablesoul.ca
https://www.instagram.com/ablesoul

About Me

My name is Lucy. I love going on adventures and particularly enjoy the outdoors; anytime I'm near the water it brings me such joy! I'm keen to try new things, including food, and I'm a lover of dark chocolate. I'm a Netflix binger (please don't judge me yet.) My friends and family are the gold nuggets that I treasure close to my heart. Most important is my love for God. By the way, I have a physical disability—cerebral palsy (CP)—hence the wheelchair on the front cover.

Some more interesting tidbits:

- I've been skydiving, water sit-skiing, horseback riding, sailing and rock climbing. Hang gliding and travelling to Australia remain on my bucket list.

- My favourite musicians are Elton John, Billy Joel and Garth Brooks. The Wow Worship series is my favourite praise music.

- My family is from Portugal and I love Portuguese food, especially my mom's cooking.

- I'm the first member of my family to earn a bachelor's degree (business administration). It took a bit longer for me, but I did it!

- Volunteering is a lifestyle practice that I value. Serving on several boards for over 28 years included being president of two non-profit organizations. It's an awesome way that I can serve my community. You could say that I'm a master of chairing meetings.

- Once I got a ride home in a paddy wagon. I was downtown when my power chair stopped working and the police came to my rescue! Not being intoxicated in any way, made the ride more memorable.

- I like to make fun of myself and often laugh at my own stupidity.

I wanted to give you a sense of who I am and hopefully you'll be able to relate on some level. None of my accomplishments would be fulfilled without God. The Lord has been with me every step of the way. He has given me grace and unconditional love to carry me through the difficult and challenging times. The following verse is my life's motto, a good reminder that there is always hope in God:

"...through whom we have gained access by faith into this grace in which we now stand. And we boast in the hope of the glory of God. Not only so, but we also glory in our sufferings, because we know that suffering produces perseverance; perseverance, character; and character, hope. And hope does not put us to shame, because God's love has been poured out into our hearts through the Holy Spirit, who has been given to us."

ROMANS 5:2-5 (NIV)

Contents

Preface

So, what led me to write this book?

This book is birthed from prayer. It is my heartfelt passion to encourage others to have a deeper connection with God's Spirit—the Holy Spirit—in everyday life.

I was recently interviewed at church for a sermon. One of the questions was: "What is the greatest barrier keeping people from living in awareness of God at every moment?" This question directly relates to why I have written this book. My answer is twofold: not continually inviting God into one's life throughout the day, and not understanding the value of time.

Since God has made us each unique, there are various approaches to prayer. As a reflective person by nature, my approach is to invite God into my life throughout my day. I typically ask him one of the following questions:

- What can I learn from this situation?

- How can I change my perspective to see through your eyes?

- Do I act now or remain quiet, waiting for your Spirit to nudge me?

If I'm not sure I hear God's voice I ask for clarification until I sense a calming in my soul. Through prayer, inviting him in on a day-to-day basis, I have discovered ways to be more receptive to the Lord.

Many people have forgotten or don't understand the value of time. Quite a few were puzzled at my response to the question at church. I said that due to my cerebral palsy, whenever I'm rushed, my involuntary movements increase causing my body to become spastic. For example, when getting on the bus, I try to be as fast as possible in parking my power chair in the designated area. Sometimes the bus driver notices that I'm having difficulty and his response is "take your time." When I hear that, my body calms down and I can park in a more efficient and timely manner.

I went on to say that this principle applies in our relationship with God as we often rush our time with him. However, when we don't take time to be with God, our souls too, can become spastic on an emotional level. Whenever a muscle spasms, it causes tension and can lead to severe pain. Therefore, the affected body part is not fully functional.

Over the years I've witnessed an overwhelming sense of oppression among faith-believers and observed many people struggling to find God in their everyday life. When we don't allow God the time to renew our souls, we tend to get stressed or overwhelmed. As a result, we are less receptive to hearing God's voice and receiving his nurture. However, when we invite God's Spirit in throughout the day, this aligns our souls with his Spirit and widens the pathway of communication.

One of the biggest challenges of living with CP is not having my voice valued and fully listened to because of my speech impediment. I live in a fast-paced society where we often forget to take the time to listen fully.

Living with a physical disability has caused me to rely on God in more ways than the average person. Like many people with disabilities, I've gained skills and tools to overcome adversity. In addressing life's roadblocks, I've learned to adapt and be open to receiving assistance from others. I've come to realize that vulnerability is a strength.

I've discovered that I work at a slower pace, especially on a physical level. It takes me longer to do things like getting dressed, using the washroom and eating a meal. The fact is, I can't maintain the pace that society demands. Through this I've also learned that God works in his own timing and that he measures time in his unique way.

These pearls of knowledge have helped me become more aware of the roadblocks in my spiritual life. I now continually pray for God's help and wisdom in navigating these barriers.

Even though my physical abilities are limited, my mind and soul are not confined by these limitations. In relying and trusting on God every day, I experience greater freedom and am able to thrive. There is a deeper contentment and an abiding peace within me.

"He gives strength to the weary and increases the power of the weak. Even youths grow tired and weary, and young men stumble and fall; but those who hope in the Lord will renew their strength. They will soar on wings like eagles; they will run and not grow weary, they will walk and not be faint."
Isaiah 40:29-31 (NIV)

In conversation with able-bodied friends, I realized they, too, feel impaired or disabled, but in different ways. This book is for everyone, as we all have challenges to overcome, whether they be physical, emotional, intellectual or spiritual. The Lord tailors how he communicates with us according to what is most beneficial to our personal listening style and circumstances. My hope is that these introspective reflections will resonate with your soul, igniting a stronger desire and will to discover ways to have holy intimacy. I pray you'll continue to build a deeper relationship with God in which you'll experience greater joy and freedom.

If you are a parent or relative of a child with a disability, I pray that you will find my life story encouraging. In spite of living with a disability, your loved one can triumph, especially with a helping hand from the Lord.

If you, yourself, are living with a disability, my hope is that you won't feel so alone. I pray that this book will give you more assurance that God is with you, especially during the challenging times. He absolutely adores you and knows your heart intimately. God will always be your cheerleader!

We learn from each other and by listening to stories. Sometimes the most powerful stories are the ones we don't experience but can relate to. They can give us a different perspective and help enlighten our minds and spirits.

I pray as you read these reflections you will find the Lord drawing you in with the warmth of his Holy Spirit.

"I pray that the eyes of your heart may be enlightened in order that you may know the hope to which he has called you, the riches of his glorious inheritance in his holy people …"
Ephesians 1:18 (NIV)

Friends

Irene McGuinness, Ginny Jaques,
Kim Pierrot, Paula & Dave Schulz,
Suzanne Paterson, Louise & Barry
Soper, Randene & Roger Hardy,
David Ducklow, Beba Morales,
Kathy Fraser, Brenda Loewen,
Matt & Rosalie
Conway

Minha Família

My mom Laurinda, brothers
Alfred & Bob, my sister Carmen
and brother-in-law Bill,
my niece Daleela &
nephew Quinton
and his wife
Rebecca.

Personal Care Team

Maureen Carrion,
Norma Tinipac,
Betty Klusmann,
Francisca Tinao,
Ross McKenzie

Scribers

June Corstorphine,
Anna Furlot,
Adrienne Mohr,
Marilina Musto

Acknowledgements

Minha Família: God has blessed me with a loving family who have learned to embrace the challenges of having a relative with a disability; never mind my adventuresome personality! It is with my utmost gratitude for their unending support and love, I thank them for their encouragement, especially in the midst of writing this book. To my mom Laurinda, thank you for your willingness to help me in any way possible, especially for the last few months, so I can finish the book. My mom makes the best Portuguese food! To my extended family in Portugal, Brazil and United States, your kind thoughts and prayers are deeply appreciated. *Obligado por tudo!*

My Hometown: Blessed to have grown up in the loving, small town of Kitimat. Please know that I haven't forgotten your kindness and I will always cherish my childhood friendships.

My Faith Communities: Capilano Christian Community Church, thank you for embracing me in my brokenness when I was so young. You gave me a strong foundation of faith and roots of love. To my present church community, C3 Vancouver, thank you for being so inclusive and for being true disciples, making the house of God accessible to all.

My Entourage: Let's face it, if it weren't for you, I'd be still in bed watching soaps. Seriously, thank you for being the extension of my hands and graciously doing all the little chores that are necessary for life to happen. It is because of you, my care attendants, I am able to live a full and productive life.

My Scribers: Countless hours of dictation—you were so patient in listening, so steadfast in asking for clarification ensuring that you type exactly what I say. You read my pages out loud and never judge when I made many revisions. Thank you for respecting my voice and not interfering in my own creative process.

My Advisors: A deep appreciation to Irene and Ginny for the editorial feedback and encouragement, as I kept feeding them chapter after chapter for them to review. Thank you for graciously volunteering your time, giving me helpful suggestions and always assuring me that I was going in the right direction. One of my mentors, Pastor Kim Pierrot was the first person to read the book in its' entirety. Thank you for respectfully guiding me, capturing my true intention of inviting the reader to contemplate their own spiritual journey with God.

My Awesome Loving Friends: You rock!!!! Thank you for being my prayerful cheerleading squad! You believed in my writing ability when I doubted myself. You stayed with me on this journey, always interested in my progress and celebrating my small milestones. You always look beyond my disability into my heart.

God is good all the time!

Prayer is the Breath of Life for Our Souls

As a Christian—a child of God—I'm passionate about the value of prayer. Maybe this is because I understand the physical implications of not having enough oxygen. At birth, the umbilical cord wrapped around my neck. For a minute or two, I did not receive any oxygen, which damaged the motor area of my brain, resulting in me having Cerebral Palsy. The type of CP I have mainly affects my speech and body mobility. I have a speech impediment and am not able to walk on my own. However, I believe that the lack of prayer has far more detrimental consequences to my soul than the physical limitations of a disability has to my body.

When we put prayer on the back burner, the oxygen to our souls begins to diminish. This can happen when we are preoccupied with the busyness of life, or when we get overwhelmed with unsettling world events. With access to news 24/7, atrocities around the world seem more daunting and times can feel scary and more discouraging. As Christians, we are in danger of being sidetracked, wondering what we can do to feed the hungry, fight against injustice and advocate for others in need. We put the onus on ourselves instead of first seeking protection and wisdom from God. Sometimes we fall into helplessness and complacency.

It seems to be more acceptable to dwell on what we ought to do to solve the problems of the world than to pray. If we try to live life and fight injustice solely on our own accord, we disconnect from God. Prayer is essential to our well-being and to the goodness of God that we need to access in order to serve humanity. Prayer can give us the "oxygen" we need to make a difference in our own lives and in the lives of others.

"Don't grieve God. Don't break his heart. **His Holy Spirit, moving and breathing in you,** *is the most intimate part of your life, making you fit for himself. Don't take such a gift for granted."*

Ephesians 4:30 (MSG) (emphasis my own)

Prayer is the breath of life for our souls. When we inhale, we receive God's grace, goodness and wisdom. When we exhale, we share our joys, concerns and other thoughts with God. Prayer is the essential act for us to create an atmosphere, to consciously make space, allowing God's Spirit to be present with us. It's a moment of intimacy where your soul can breathe and God's Spirit can connect with your heart and mind.

"Those who are motivated by the flesh only pursue what benefits themselves. But those who live by the impulses of the Holy Spirit are motivated to pursue spiritual realities. For the mind-set of the flesh is death, but the mind-set controlled by the Spirit finds life and peace."

ROMANS 8:5-6 (TPT)

Through the power of prayer, we can be more receptive to God's anointing, allowing us to be freer as we cope with everyday life and when we do acts of service. In our personal relationship with the Lord, prayer is the substance of the divine connection which propels the real nourishment into our souls.

Although the effects from the lack of prayer in one's life are not as visibly noticeable as the lack of oxygen to me with my disability, they can still wreak havoc on one's emotional and mental state. Thankfully, with God it is never too late to inhale and allow his Spirit to resuscitate our souls with his goodness.

Dear Heavenly Father,

Thank you, Lord, for being a Father who is always present in every circumstance that we face. I'm in awe of your endless capacity for patience, love and grace.

You are the living water that quenches my thirsty soul; you are the anchor that keeps me afloat even through the roughest waves. Your Holy Spirit is like a blanket that warms my soul, keeping me secure and enclosed in your divine protection.

Lord, I confess, at times I do put our relationship on the back burner, especially when I feel overwhelmed or preoccupied with the demands of life. It's so easy to get lost in the busyness that I forget to take a few moments to be in your presence. Time with you is so precious, so essential for our relationship and my rejuvenation.

May I take time to allow your Holy Spirit to breathe into my daily life. When I get overwhelmed by life's worries, may I bring them to you and ask for your discernment.

May I be refuelled in the joy of being in your presence, knowing that you are my strength, that I can take comfort in you, and that you will guide me when needed.

Help me remember that spending time with you brings you joy, as well. May the souls of my brothers and sisters in Christ also be refreshed as they take time to breathe in your presence.

Thank you, Holy Spirit, for being the oxygen for our souls, continuously filling us with your sustenance, and revitalizing our souls and minds.

Amen

Come take a few moments to rest in the Spirit. Let God help you untangle the cord of stress wrapped around your spirit. Breathe in and allow the Lord to resuscitate your soul.

God is Always Accessible

*L*ack of accessibility is one of the challenges I face living with a disability. In terms of physical accessibility, I use a power chair to navigate around. Even though accessibility in the Greater Vancouver area of British Columbia has greatly improved over the years, it is still limited for people with disabilities. There have been times when I've attended a meeting or social function where the meeting place was inaccessible. Either there were stairs outside the building or no elevator to get to the correct floor. There have also been times when I've had to motor on the road because there was no curb ramp to access the sidewalk. Furthermore, ninety percent of my friends' homes are not wheelchair accessible, so we meet at my place or in a coffee shop.

Another challenge in terms of accessibility has to do with how others view me. I have a speech impediment, which sometimes makes people hesitant to talk with me.

They are afraid they won't understand me, or they don't have the time to listen. For the most part I can be understood and once you are acquainted with my speech patterns it becomes less of a barrier. It just takes a bit of time and patience. This has been an ongoing obstacle for me, especially in my pursuit of employment opportunities.

However, it's a completely different experience with God. He's always fully accessible and an excellent listener. It's a totally different world with him, which I enjoy immensely! I never have to wonder how receptive he will be. I don't have to climb any stairs or prove my intelligence. With him, I am free to be myself. God doesn't put up any barriers.

"And now, because we are united to Christ, we both have equal and direct access in the realm of the Holy Spirit to come before the Father!"
Ephesians 2:18 (TPT)

Unfortunately, I'm the one who puts up the barriers with my emotions or unwillingness. But the beauty of having a disability is that I have learned to let go—to become more open to the Holy Spirit and rely more on God's strength, as it is far more resilient than mine.

The best part is that we all have equal access to him and to the blessings of his anointed Spirit.

God is Always Accessible

Dear Father in Heaven,

One of the attributes I most admire about you is how accessible you are to everyone. There are no mountains to climb, no bureaucratic regulations to follow or hoops to jump through to reach you, Lord. All we need to do is unlock our hearts and let you in.

> *"We have boldness through him [our Lord Jesus Christ], and free access as kings before the Father because of our complete confidence in Christ's faithfulness."*
>
> EPHESIANS 3:12 (TPT)

You are ever present, graciously waiting for us to meet you. Thank you for making your Spirit inclusive, accessible to everybody, despite our level of ability, intelligence or emotional well-being.

You constantly invite us to come to you as we are, accepting our frailties, and you eagerly wait to show us your healing power and divine wisdom.

I pray that we can all embrace the simplicity of being in a relationship with you and not allow your love to be overshadowed by religious complications or humanly manufactured unworthiness. Thank you, Lord, for being a loving Father to all.

Amen

You have free reign to love and be loved by God. What are some of the barriers that you need God to help you remove so you can be more intimate with his Spirit?

Don't Cover Up
Your Mess

*L*iving with a disability gives me a unique perspective that a lot of people may not experience but might be able to relate to. This perspective has helped shape my faith and deepen my intimate relationship with the Lord, and is one of the many reasons that inspired me to write this book. A valuable truth I've gained from having a disability is that I need to accept my circumstances, my appearance and my messy way of doing things. I've learned how to be more authentic and not be concerned so much about exterior appearances or prestige.

With having CP, the messages in the motor area of my brain can be misdirected temporarily, so I often experience involuntary body movements when I engage in concentrated physical activity. As a consequence, when I feed myself, it can get really messy. When my arm wavers sporadically, pieces of food can slide off the spoon, onto the table or even land on the floor. Imagine a toddler feeding herself and you get the picture, minus the temper tantrums, of course.

I remember once when I was in a café eating a piece of chocolate cake, an acquaintance stopped by to say hello. I had remnants of cake on my face and cheeks, so I automatically pulled my arm up to cover my mouth because I felt embarrassed and ashamed. I didn't want to gross them out.

What does this have to do with our relationship with God? In some respects, we all hide parts of ourselves from God: our weaknesses, our imperfections, our sins and our sorrows. The issue here is that we build up walls, blocking out areas of our hearts, making it harder for God to come in.

"You're blessed when you're at the end of your rope. With less of you there is more of God and his rule. You're blessed when you feel you've lost what is most dear to you. Only then can you be embraced by the One most dear to you.
You're blessed when you're content with just who you are—no more, no less. That's the moment you find yourselves proud owners of everything that can't be bought."

MATTHEW 5:3-5 (MSG)

I learned at a young age—and am still reminding myself to accept—that my appearance might not always be appealing to others. For me, prestige is not so significant that it would prevent me from going out to have a bite to eat, socializing at a party or just enjoying a scrumptious piece of cake. Hunger and companionship prevail over beauty.

That is also what is required with God in order to have deeper intimacy with him. Sometimes we wonder why we can't hear God, feel his Holy Spirit or enjoy his presence. We tend to keep up walls of shame and live by our pretences, which makes it harder to let the Spirit in and allow God to bless us. By accepting our imperfections and releasing the negative thoughts, we free up space so that the Lord can come in and be the sanctuary to quiet our souls.

Dear Heavenly Father,

It will take my lifetime to completely accept my frailties and imperfections, especially the ones that I can't change. Continuing to be upset or discouraged over them is rather pointless and can distract me from opportunities and blessings that you may put forth.

Able Soul

Lord, I confess that I have a habit of straying away from you when I am emotionally distraught. Especially in times when I'm discouraged, I often feel unworthy of your love, and that I need to be in better spirits and grateful for what I have. In times like these, I realize I need to lean on you more as you always have a way of changing my perspective or providing a piece of wisdom that I need in that moment.

Lord we are blessed with the ability to accept what we can't change and the knowledge that you, Oh Lord, accept us where we are. You can take our weaknesses and use them to your advantage.

How wonderful to understand that you are the master creator who can tweak, remold and adapt to our quirks.

Amen

Look at your reflection in the mirror. Imagine God behind you, lovingly gazing over your shoulder. What can you do to release shame and accept God's grace?

Changing Indicators

With any type of vehicle, a dashboard is the main control panel. This is where all the controls and indicators are, such as the fuel gauge, speedometer and gearshift, which determine the way you drive. We rely on such indicators to control our vehicles and ensure they function properly and precisely.

To manoeuvre my vehicle (power chair) I use a joystick, which also has a monitor. Similar to a dashboard, my monitor shows me which drive setting I'm in (indoor/outdoor/aggressive), my rate of speed and the amount of charge in my battery.

One time the monitor on my joystick control panel went completely blank. I couldn't see any of the gauges. Imagine if any of the indicators on your car dashboard stopped working. What would you do? Of course, for safety reasons you would be obligated to stop using the vehicle until it's repaired.

I have an advantage. If my monitor goes blank, I still have the luxury of being able to continue driving my power chair using alternate indicators.

For example, I have a dial button on the control box that reflects my speed. If the white dot is toward the left, it means I'm going at a slower pace. I can manually turn the dial button to change the speed.

In terms of selecting the drive or gear, it beeps each time the drive button is pressed. Hence, I can count the beeps to determine which drive I'm in. I can also tell from my driving experience how fast the power chair is going. Therefore, by using my other senses to gauge my chair, I can avoid being stranded at home and continue with my activities.

Now, what the heck does this have to do with our relationship with God?

One of the greatest challenges we all have in our faith is listening. We get used to listening to God in a certain way, following certain cues we have come to depend on. When we are not able to pick up on these familiar indicators, we grow impatient, give up in defeat and stop praying as we think God is silent or not speaking at all.

But what's so magnificent about God is that he uses various communication styles and techniques to draw us to him. We forget that we have different senses that we can utilize.

Perhaps the next time we think we can't hear God, or that he isn't listening, maybe we need to change our perspective and go beyond our usual indicators. Let's open our minds to other ways God communicates and exercise all of our senses so we can truly comprehend his message and receive his blessing to the full extent.

"Teach me more about you, how you work and how you move, so that I can walk onward in your truth until everything within me brings honor to your name."

PSALM 86:11 (TPT)

Dear Father in Heaven,

How easy it is to get caught up in the routine of life. I can get into a rut of doing things in the same manner and forget to look beyond my usual ways, especially in the area of listening to you and seeking your wisdom.

I confess that I get frustrated when I don't find you answering my prayers in ways that I'm accustomed. It's hypocritical of me, especially when I ask you to refresh my mind or renew my soul. Sometimes I forget what I'm really asking for and what that entails.

Able Soul

Forgive me for my absentmindedness and my selfish ways, as I can get blindsided by my own expectations of how you will answer me. Teach me to be more adaptable in listening to your Holy Spirit. May I also be more receptive when listening to others and respectful of their style of communication.

Thank you, Lord, for always responding to my prayers in ways that are more beneficial to my soul than what I believe I need.

Amen

God enjoys romancing your soul. He knows your love language and delights in surprising you in dynamic ways. Close your eyes, clear your mind and enjoy the courtship of the Lord.

God to My Rescue

"If you say, "The Lord is my refuge," and you make the Most High your dwelling, no harm will overtake you, no disaster will come near your tent. For he will command his angels concerning you to guard you in all your ways; they will lift you up in their hands, so that you will not strike your foot against a stone."

PSALM 91:9-12 (NIV)

As a young adult, I was a bit spontaneous and sometimes this led me into precarious situations where God had to intervene. One event especially comes to mind: a trip to a concert at the University of British Columbia. I had arranged to meet my date there. Before the concert I went sailing at Jericho Beach with the Disabled Sailing Association. Since the beach was close to the university and I had ample time, instead of taking the bus, I decided to motor in my power chair, not being aware of the actual distance or terrain.

The university is located on a peninsula at the top of a hill. I proceeded along the seawall to the hill and as the trip become much longer than I had anticipated, I confirmed with people walking by that I was still headed in the right direction. Upon reaching the hill I had two options: I could either travel on the street or take the gravel path parallel to the road that was separated by a cement barricade. Unsure how much traffic there would be, I decided the safest bet was to take the trail.

As I ventured on the rocky pathway, I noticed it was getting narrower and I felt like I was driving my chair on a tightrope. I cautiously maneuvered the joystick to avoid any sharp turns and to keep my balance. Since I was very nervous and focused on the trail, I failed to look up and enjoy the beauty of the surrounding forest; however, I did peek sideways and noticed the downward slope beside the path. My nerves began to fray, my stomach kept turning and my heart was pounding. There was no room to turn my chair around and head back. Even though I was afraid of what lay ahead, I kept motoring forward, taking deep breaths to remain calm.

All of a sudden, my back tire hit a rock and my chair flipped sideways. The impact startled me as I fell on my right side causing a jolt of pain in my arm. My head was hanging over the cliff with my shoulder leaning against the edge. There was a waterfall trickling below. I started getting dizzy from the blood rushing to my head.

I began sliding farther toward the edge. Any kind of jerking motion would make my chair slide down faster. Tree branches surrounded me and I managed to grab one. At that moment, I felt a sense of peace and calm like I was wrapped in a warm blanket. I wasn't afraid.

I started praying to God. The kind of conversation you have when your life is about to end. I told him how blessed I was and what a great life I'd had. I asked him to take care of my family and friends and to forgive me for my stupidity.

My chair kept sliding and my head inched farther over the edge. Astonishingly, a man from out of nowhere grabbed my chair and stopped it! Caught by surprise, I tried to figure out what was happening. He managed to hold my chair and keep it from sliding off the cliff while recruiting some other guys to help. I have no clue how he did it as the combined weight of me plus my chair is over 300 pounds. I truly believe he was an angel because I didn't see anybody on the path in any direction.

The rescue team pulled me back to an upright position. Then they lifted me and my chair over the cement barricade onto the road. It happened so quickly that it took me a minute to reconfigure my body and composure. With the acknowledgment of my utmost and deepest gratitude, we parted ways.

I arrived at the concert hall without any further drama or pitfalls and enjoyed a lovely evening with my handsome young man.

It's been over twenty years since this adventure occurred. I still marvel at God's grace over me. It's awesome that God's protection allows us to embrace the unexpected—especially the angels.

Dear Father in Heaven,

As I reminisce about the countless ways that you have come to my rescue I get overwhelmed with a sense of freedom.

You are my saving grace. You allow me to walk fearlessly and to embrace life to the fullest. Your love for me has blessed me with unbounded security, knowing that when I fall, I can trust you to give me a helping hand.

Lord, let us be courageous in our obedience to do your will, to stand up for injustice in the face of oppression and to be compassionate in place of judgement. Whenever we fail, let us not be ruled by shame but lean into your everlasting grace.

Amen

God has a safety net around you. What is your holy 911 story?

A Mothering Dream

"'For I know the plans I have for you,' declares the
LORD, *'plans to prosper you and not to harm you,*
plans to give you hope and a future.'"
JEREMIAH 29:11 (NIV)

I once told a friend that I like to dream big, beyond
my own capacity, because it's the only way to
ensure that I'm inviting and including God in my life.
One particular dream that I have always held close to my
heart is having children. Not biologically, but through
fostering or adoption.

My perception of the dream has changed as I've
matured and reality has set in. In my young adulthood

I wanted to foster children, but I failed to meet the eligibility criteria of financial and physical ability. Being a practical person, I knew I didn't have the capability to look after a baby or a toddler, but perhaps I could care for a child of eight years of age or older. I also researched the possibility of adoption, but the process is complicated and expensive.

Now in my forties, my desire to support children in need of a safe, loving home has deepened. The scope of my dream has expanded. I now imagine a residential complex full of renters who help support kids whether they need respite care, fostering or adoption. It would be a communal place, so people like myself could help families support their children.

Sometimes our quest to fight injustice derives from overcoming adversity. My passion to help kids stems from my own personal experience of living in foster care. My situation was unique because my mother, who loved me wholeheartedly, could not meet my physical needs by herself. My father had died from cancer when I was three, leaving my mom a single parent of four young children, including one with a disability. At the time I was living in a residential hospital for children in Vancouver. After four years in the hospital, the medical staff decided that I would thrive in a home environment closer to my family. When I was eight, I returned to my hometown and moved into a foster home. I was so happy to be near my birth family once again.

I loved my foster mother and foster sisters and enjoyed attending their church. My relationship with the Lord became more real as I opened up my heart and committed my life to Jesus. However, unbeknownst to my mother and foster mother, my foster father sexually abused me on a regular basis during the four years that I stayed with them. God carried me through this darkest and most painful time of my childhood.

This experience is where my passion to help protect children comes from. I understand some of the challenges that they may have experienced and, of course, I hope no child has to endure any kind of abuse.

In order to heal my heart, I needed God's help. Through his divine intervention, he blessed me with the gift of forgiveness. Similarly, in my dream to foster children in need, I must trust God to fulfill my wishes according to his will and vision. I realize that my own imagination is miniscule compared to God's.

While I accept that my desire to follow in the footsteps of my loving mother and have children of my own will never diminish, I realize that dream is not mine to hold on to. It's easy to get stuck in our own dreams and wonder why God hasn't yet allowed them to come to fruition. However, if we trust him, God can take our hearts' desires and longings and mold them for a greater purpose.

Able Soul

Dear Father in Heaven,

There's so much I would like to do, so many people to help, kids to nurture and protect, social injustices to right. Never mind the places where I'd like to travel or the adventures on my bucket list—and I'm always coming up with new ideas.

The awesome part is that I don't need to complete them by myself. I remember in my younger days how I would get so disappointed and frustrated when something that I really wanted didn't happen, but yet, you remained patient and faithful, creating opportunities that were best suited for my gifts and abilities and more favourable to bless others, including myself.

I keep dreaming beyond my capacity, believing that you will take my hopes and ideas and make me an instrument of peace and divine love, a light of your radiant kindness and a means of displaying the graciousness of your love.

Lord, keep putting each one of us in places where your holy reflection can shine brightly. We are blessed knowing that you are the one who takes our wishes and from them designs a tapestry of love and grace that blesses humankind.

"Keep trusting in the Lord and do what is right in his eyes. Fix your heart on the promises of God and you will be secure, feasting on his faithfulness. Make God the utmost delight and pleasure of your life, and he will provide for you what you desire the most. Give God the right to direct your life, and as you trust him along the way you'll find he pulled it off perfectly!"

PSALM 37:3-5 (TPT)

Amen

Remember a dream or desire that God has brought into fruition. Now think about one that has yet to be fulfilled. Daydream with God and imagine the possibilities with him.

The Basics of Life—
Forgiveness

*I*n my early twenties, one particular worship song that resonated with my soul was called "The Basics of Life" by 4Him. This song struck a chord with me as my love for Christ deepened and I started longing for emotional healing from my childhood. In order to mature in my faith, I asked God to help me remove barriers that were preventing me from experiencing the fullness of grace with a pure heart.

The chorus says:

> *We need to get back*
> *To the basics of life*
> *A heart that is pure*
> *And a love that is blind*
> *A faith that is fervently*
> *Grounded in Christ*
> *The hope that endures for all times*
> *These are the basics.*
> *We need to get back*
> *To the basics of life*

Today, considering the magnitude of anger and hate disseminated around the world, especially on social media, these lyrics are so relevant. How do we return to a state of unconditional love and deep abiding peace?

As I contemplated these lyrics in my early twenties, I wondered how I could love unconditionally and make my heart pure, without resentment.

Forgiveness.

At that point in my life I felt like an emotionless zombie. I kept having a reoccurring dream that I was stabbing someone with a knife. I didn't understand the purpose of the dream until I heard this song and was confronted by how stagnant my heart was. Through prayer God showed me that I was still burdened by painful experiences from my childhood.

I needed to address the fact that I was in survival mode and had repressed post-traumatic stress from the sexual abuse that occurred in my foster home. Even though at age fourteen I made the decision to forgive my offender, I was too young to understand that I would also need to deal with the long-term ramifications of the trauma.

Forgiveness is a process; it doesn't happen overnight, rather, it happens in stages. Depending on the offence, it can take time for the heart to heal and connect with your mind in agreement toward forgiveness.

Just as I prayed to receive God's forgiveness for my own mistakes, I also needed to ask him for the grace to forgive. I couldn't do it completely on my own. I had to pray multiple times to ask God to change my heart.

Throughout the years, even though I had moved past the abuse, the memories of my offender crept up once in a while. I kept wondering what had happened to him.

A few years ago, I finally had the courage to seek the answer. I found out that he had been given a second chance at redemption—to be reunited with his family—but he lost it. That moment of revelation was so profound as my heart was filled with compassion and sadness for his family.

The fact that I experienced empathy and grace was the last piece of the puzzle that I needed to confirm that I had completely forgiven him. Forgiveness was the key for me in finally unlocking my heart and making more room for God's Spirit. This process allowed me to enjoy a deeper sense of holy love and kindness. It solidified that I was no longer a prisoner of past hurts, but instead I was a captive of holy grace, free to love.

"Get rid of all bitterness, rage and anger, brawling and slander, along with every form of malice. Be kind and compassionate to one another, forgiving each other, just as in Christ God forgave you."
EPHESIANS 4:31-32 (NIV)

Able Soul

Dear Father in Heaven,

Sometimes I forget to treasure the value of forgiveness, how it is the foundation of our relationship with you, Lord. You have forgiven me countless times for acts of selfishness, wrongdoing against others and my own ignorance.

It's heartbreaking for me to realize that in today's world we have lost the culture of forgiving others, becoming less tolerant and more hostile. Lord, I pray that everyone can experience the grace and mercy that you bestowed on me, as well as on my brothers and sisters in Christ.

I'm so grateful that I'm free from past hurts. By your grace I'm free to love, to see people through your eyes and to have compassion when others offend me.

Martin Luther King, Jr. said, "Forgiveness is not an occasional act. It is a permanent attitude." Lord, I pray that we can all develop a similar attitude to that which you have toward us. May we turn to you with our hurts instead of getting caught up in revengeful thoughts.

May we continue to treat others with dignity even through the times of persecution and rejection.

May we strive to walk with confidence, reflecting your mercy, and know by grace we are forgiven and by your grace we can forgive others.

In your holy name,
Amen

 Forgiveness is an avenue for God to help heal your brokenness. How have you experienced being captured by holy grace?

Loose Connections

*A*s with any vehicle, breakdowns or malfunctions are bound to happen to my power chair. One particular malfunction happened during the season of Lent, which, interestingly, gave me an insightful revelation.

For a few days I was driving my power chair with an error message that kept flashing on the monitor of my joystick control box. The sign displayed a yellow triangle with an exclamation mark. The error message read "bad cable."

I had my assistant check out the cables and wires for a loose connection but she couldn't find any. My power chair is my main source of transportation and allows me a lot of independence. It's hard for me to use a manual chair on my own. I called the wheelchair repair service and waited for a callback.

Meanwhile, I decided to proceed as I usually do, attend meetings, go grocery shopping, etc. The error message was always in the back of my mind and I was conscious of the fact that my chair could stop working at any time, but I continued with my daily activities.

In life we often continue to function, in our jobs, with our families, playing sports, doing activities or attending church, all while sensing a nagging feeling or a void indicating that something is missing. We have an internal error message that we tend to ignore or put on hold. Perhaps we need more time with God—more intimacy—so we can have a stronger connection and hear him more clearly.

One of the purposes of prayer is to check in with God, to evaluate our relationship with him and find out if we have any loose connections. Lent, in particular, is a time to fine-tune our listening skills and to ask God to help us connect with him on a deeper level.

"So you must remain in life-union with me, for I remain in life-union with you. For as a branch severed from the vine will not bear fruit, so your life will be fruitless unless you live your life intimately joined to mine."

JOHN 15:4 (TPT)

Unlike the situation with my power chair where I needed to wait for a repairman, we don't need to wait to fix our internal error message. God is always present, waiting for us to invite him in, to help tidy up any loose connections, to affirm his love and to pour out his grace.

Dear Father in Heaven,

I feel a bit discombobulated. My mind and ears are not fully in tune with your Holy Spirit. I sense a void in my soul signalling to me that something is out of alignment.

The longer I ignore it the more distant I feel from you. Please forgive me for straying away. Thank you for your patience and for always leaving the door open.

I ask you, oh Lord, to reveal what I need to change. Help me to solder any loose connections. Bind all of us closer to you.

May we not ignore any internal error messages, as they help to guide us in evaluating our inner being and to check in with your Holy Spirit.

Amen

The Lord is your soul's handyman. When you have an internal error message or sense a disconnection from God, ask God to spark your soul with his grace.

Honouring the Intent of Communion

"*Simply join your life with mine. Learn my ways and you'll discover that I'm gentle, humble, easy to please. You will find refreshment and rest in me.*"
MATTHEW 11:29 (TPT)

I always look forward to communion at church. I never get tired of the tradition—a sacred act that honours God and replenishes our souls. Sometimes I wonder who delights in it more, Jesus or myself.

The representation of the Body of Christ as bread, and his blood as wine, humanizes the deep, compassionate, unending love of God. To be invited to his table as we are, full of human frailties, is an enormous, heartfelt gift.

One aspect of communion that is rarely talked about or encouraged is the value of being vulnerable—letting your guard down, coming as your true self, despite the emotional state you may be in, without self-condemnation or the false necessity to put on a façade of strength and joy. When we mask parts of our emotional complexion, we rob ourselves from fully receiving God's blessing and anointing.

In some respects, I feel I have an advantage compared to my brothers and sisters in Christ. Every time I'm invited out to dinner or to a party, I need someone to assist me with eating. When I was in my late teens, I would feel uncomfortable asking for help as I didn't want to feel like a burden or bother anyone. Sometimes, I would leave a party without eating anything, which defeated the purpose and left me hungry.

In this case, wisdom prevailed as I matured not only in age but also in self-confidence. I learned to let go of my pride and inhibitions. My perspective has completely changed. I'm no longer embarrassed, nor do I feel like a burden. Sometimes I have even asked a complete stranger for assistance at a party. I use this to my advantage as a means of socializing and getting to know that person.

One of the things I value about communion is that we are all identical in the eyes of the Holy Spirit. Although, unlike myself, you may physically be able to feed yourself the bread and wine, we are not able to feed our souls alone. In communion, we are all equally dependent on Jesus to nourish our souls.

"Are you weary, carrying a heavy burden? Then come to me. I will refresh your life, for I am your oasis. Simply join your life with mine. Learn my ways and you'll discover that I'm gentle, humble, easy to please. You will find refreshment and rest in me. For all that I require of you will be pleasant and easy to bear."

MATTHEW 11:28-30 (TPT)

From my life experience, I have developed the assuredness of being comfortable with coming to Jesus as who I am with all my imperfections. I gladly accept being dependent on him to feed my soul.

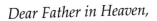

Dear Father in Heaven,

The act of communion is so sacred, a tradition that invites us to enter into your presence. A gift bestowed to us to allow our spirits to be restored with your grace and mercy. A moment where our spirits can be harmonized with you in an intimate community.

I confess that sometimes I have fallen into complacency, not always being fully open and appreciating the sacredness and luxury of participating in communion. Lord, please forgive me for taking this act for granted.

Thank you for this sacred tradition and the invitation to all of us to come as we are despite our frailties, a reminder that you are the only one that can bring restoration and peace to our souls.

Amen

Next time you're invited to come for communion, envision Jesus looking at you with his doting, loving eyes, full of anticipation, rising to greet you. Imagine he's prepared a table full of decadent food, especially for you, knowing what you personally require to rejuvenate your own soul.

All you need to do is be your true self and come to the table.

My Heavenly Realtor

*W*hat is your favourite reality show? One of my guilty pleasures is watching house-hunting shows. I enjoy observing the human behaviour aspect. There is usually a difference of opinion between the house hunter and the realtor.

Every prospective buyer has a slate of must-haves and wishes regarding their new home. When the realtor shows them a place that doesn't meet all their requirements, they are usually reluctant to see it. However, the realtor may have a broader perspective and believe that the house could be a good fit for them. After looking at the place, the buyer is able to understand the rationale of the real estate agent.

I had a similar experience when applying for accessible housing. Even though I didn't get to select my suite, I still presented a slate of wishes to my heavenly realtor. In my case, the must-have was a wheelchair-friendly suite.

This included a wheel-in shower, wider hallways and lower counters, stovetop, light switches and electrical outlets.

Besides the necessary features, my wish list included having easy access in and out of my apartment. I prayed for a ground floor unit as I thought it would be less hassle than using the elevator. Like the house hunter, when I didn't get everything I wanted and was assigned to a suite on the second floor, I was a bit disappointed. But I was still excited to be living on my own.

"Go ahead and make all the plans you want, but it's the Lord who will ultimately direct your steps. We are all in love with our own opinions, convinced they're correct. But the Lord is in the midst of us, testing and probing our every motive. Before you do anything, put your trust totally in God and not in yourself. Then every plan you make will succeed."
Proverbs 16:1-3 (TPT)

Nearly twenty years later I'm still grateful that God had the wisdom to ignore my ill-informed wish list. My apartment unit is absolutely suited to my needs. My heavenly realtor also accounted for features that I had not considered but he knew I would fully enjoy. My suite is spacious, and the building has an open-concept garden walkway and a secondary entrance easily accessed by my care attendants.

God foresaw the obstacles that I would encounter living on the ground floor. He knew it would be difficult for me to buzz in my assistants and he knew the parameters that my power chair requires to maneuver inside small living spaces. God provided a safe accessible home where I'm thriving!

The concept of surrendering my heart's desires to God and including his will in my plans took me years to integrate and embrace. Being a person of perseverance and determination, I had to learn to relinquish the need to be in control and to trust the Lord with my plans. Even though I'm happily single with a mind of my own, I'm also gladly committed to following the path that God has set out. God always wants us to share our personal dreams and hopes with him. He also asks us to be open to his plans in accordance with his will and timing.

Dear Father in Heaven,

You must keep rolling your eyes at me. "How long will it take for her to figure it out? How many times do I have to remind her that I know what is best—that my timing is perfect?"

I, too, am mystified by my own dense mind. Why does it take me so long to clue in? How many times do I need to make the same mistake before I learn?

It's challenging to break away from my innate learned behaviour. Most of my life I've relied on self-determination and perseverance to accomplish my goals. Now, waiting upon your guidance, Lord, calls for me to change my independent ways. As I become more reliant on your Spirit, I have greater freedom to be myself and thrive.

Lord, take all of our aspirations, heart's desires and wish lists melding them into your plans. May we not be carried away with single-mindedness, but be more receptive to your holy insight. In times of waiting, let us be steadfast in remembering how gracious you've been in responding to our personal dreams and prayers. May our visions become aligned with yours.

Amen

The Lord is the ultimate problem solver and ingenious at meeting your desires. Think of an aspiration or dream that has been fulfilled with the helping hand of God. How has God blessed that dream? Invite his Spirit to keep dreaming with you.

Blessed in the Produce Store

Grocery shopping is a challenge for me. Throughout the years, I've mastered a way to collect items by having the shopping basket on my lap, dragging products to the edge of the shelf, and letting them fall into the basket. This was a way I could manage on my own. I had it down to a fine art, until recently when stores began replacing the hand-held baskets with the new rolling carts.

This began in the large stores but now has expanded everywhere. I couldn't avoid the new system any longer. In fact, on one of my shopping runs, I got so discouraged that I was overcome by tears in the store. I felt robbed of that tiny bit of independence that most people take for granted. I just wanted to get my produce without so much hassle.

I had a minute of self-pity, questioning why able-bodied people need everything to be easier. Seriously, how difficult is it to carry a shopping basket? Are people getting lazy?

After my momentary release of frustration, I left in pursuit of another store where they still had the old baskets. A few blocks down there was a produce store which, to my glee, still had the baskets that I could carry on my lap. I managed to get most of the items on my list when a fellow shopper came up to me and said, "I see you struggling to get some of your produce. May I help you?" She had a delightful English accent and a very sweet nature. Not being one to refuse a kind offer, I accepted.

She helped me get the remaining items on my list. I told her how much I appreciated her assistance. She asked if she could assist me every couple of weeks with groceries as she could see how challenging it was for me. Her generosity and confidence to ask me was so astounding. I replied, "Are you sure?" and she said yes, so I gave her my email address.

Regardless if she didn't follow up, I was so touched that God would intervene in this small capacity. I know he saw my tears. I still needed to figure out a viable way to shop on my own, but this time I didn't have to because I received a heavenly reprieval.

"You are so intimately aware of me, Lord. You read my heart like an open book and you know all the words I'm about to speak before I even start a

sentence! You know every step I will take before my journey even begins. You've gone into my future to prepare the way, and in kindness you follow behind me to spare me from the harm of my past. With your hand of love upon my life, you impart a blessing to me. This is just too wonderful, deep, and incomprehensible! Your understanding of me brings me wonder and strength."

Psalms 139: 3-6 (TPT)

We often forget that God cares about the small details. I think, in this case, he wanted to remind me that I'm not alone, that he has my back. This is why I love him so. God is the only and best Heavenly Father that we could ever have.

Dear Father in Heaven,

How marvelous of you to intercede on my behalf. What a gift it is to know that you are walking by my side, sharing my struggle and lending a helping hand as a token of love—a friendly reminder that you are guiding my path and that when we try our best you will take care of the rest.

When I'm failing, or about to fail, thank you for being patient with me during my moments of self-pity and allowing me time to regroup. Thank you, Lord, for instilling in me an inner confidence to keep striving to do what I can and believing everything will work out, as your grace is in the midst.

Thank you, Lord, for knowing us all intimately, for finding ways to ease our struggles and for lifting our spirits up to fly on your heavenly wings.

Amen

God is the ultimate parent. He always has your back, lifting you onto his shoulders when you least expect it.

Swollen Feet: A Reminder to Be Steadfast

I am a sun goddess. My favourite season is summer because I don't have to worry about all the fuss of putting on a jacket or rain gear, which can be labour intensive. I enjoy the freedom of travelling with the sun beaming on my face.

One summer, I noticed that my feet had started to swell. At first, I ignored them as I felt no pain and believed eventually the swelling would lessen. A week later, the swelling worsened and migrated up to my knees, causing my knees to become like melons!

I grew concerned and started researching online, only to discover the long-term implications. If my feet remained swollen, they could be prone to infection or blood clots. I realized I had to take this more seriously by following treatment and preventative measures. I elevated my feet, drank more water and in lieu of the suggestion of increased walking, I moved my legs around to stimulate the circulation. By taking these steps, the swelling eventually diminished. In the future, I will need to be more conscientious and proactive regarding my legs and feet.

Proverbs 3:5 reminds us to "Trust in the Lord with all your heart and lean not on your own understanding." This verse often stands alone in people's minds. However, as you continue reading, verse 6 says: "In all your ways submit to him, and he will make your paths straight." Just as we take preventative measures to keep our body healthy, we need to have the same mind-set with our souls' well-being. As this Scripture indicates, it is imperative we stay connected to the Lord by honouring him and seeking his wisdom.

In our relationship with God, we can experience dry seasons where we feel distant from him. During these times, feelings of emptiness, restlessness, numbness or frustration can occur, setting off internal indicators that our spiritual well-being is not fully in tune with the Holy Spirit. Instead of suppressing these emotions, we need to acknowledge our feelings and remove roadblocks which hinder us from experiencing God's love, thus promoting spiritual health and intimacy. The remedy for safeguarding our relationship with the Lord is to remain mindful and steadfast in seeking God's wisdom. That in itself will bring healing and refreshment to our souls.

"Do not be wise in your own eyes; fear the Lord and shun evil. This will bring health to your body and nourishment to your bones."

PROVERBS 3: 7-8 (NIV)

Dear Father in Heaven,

"Where are you Lord?" I say this sometimes when I feel distant from you. In my head I know you are present but there is a feeling of disconnection.

There are times when I don't hear your voice for a while, as I'm preoccupied with my own baggage or emotional distress. I fail to spend time with you, seeking your wisdom and enjoying your presence.

Please forgive me for my lack of attentiveness. Be patient with me, Lord, for I am so in love with you. My desire is to remain close to you.

Able Soul

Thank you for loving me through my emotional valleys and always giving me a way back to you. May I be steadfast in loving you all of my days.

Amen

 What are some of your remedies to keep your spiritual well-being healthy and heavenly?

Cageless Being

*I*n life we all face personal battles. Some are caused by our own doing and some are inflicted by society's prejudices. These unwarranted judgements or preconceived notions can hinder our self-esteem. As a person growing up with a physical disability, I often felt like my soul was trapped in a cage because of the constant need to prove myself. Like everyone, I have things that I wish I could change about myself. But honestly, I've never wished that I didn't have CP. At least I have a valid reason for not doing the dishes! However, I do wish more people would see me as a complete, whole person.

Growing up with a disability is challenging at any time. In the 1970s, people were only beginning to become more accepting and inclusive toward those with disabilities. Nonetheless, as a child with CP, I was often

discriminated against because of my physical appearance and speech impediment, instead of being noticed
for my level of intelligence or delightful personality!
Typically, in the first encounter, people were unsure how
to act toward me. They would talk in a slow and loud
manner or they would talk to the person beside me. My
automatic response was to make them feel comfortable
and prove my level of intelligence by answering their
questions. Because of my innate desire for everyone,
including myself, to be treated as an equal, a burden
of advocacy was birthed in me to help close the gap of
ignorance.

Spending four years of my childhood in a children's
hospital gave me a deeper appreciation of my capa-
bilities. I lived with some kids who were paralyzed or
were unable to verbally communicate. Although a bit
lonely, this living situation blessed me with a sense of
diligence; it instilled in me a deep motivation to always
try my best, to go beyond my perceived limitations and
find creative solutions to accomplish the tasks ahead
of me.

I remember during my teens people prayed over
me for healing. I felt awkward as they were praying
for me to have the ability to walk, to become more like
them—to become able-bodied. Although they had the
best of intentions, this kind of prayer left me feeling
like I wasn't a whole person or good enough as I was.
The last time a person asked to pray for my physical
healing I politely declined, informing the person that I

didn't need to be healed—that I was perfectly content having a disability and was blessed to know that God loves me unconditionally!

"So I will celebrate my weaknesses, for when I'm weak I sense more deeply the mighty power of Christ living in me. So I'm not defeated by my weakness, but delighted! For when I feel my weakness and endure mistreatment—when I'm surrounded with troubles on every side and face persecution because of my love for Christ—I am made yet stronger. For my weakness becomes a portal to God's power."

2 Corinthians 12:9b-10 (TPT)

Dealing with societal prejudices on your own can take an emotional toll. In my case, after years of enduring this, I felt like my soul was trapped and this led me to a couple of significant meltdowns.

Once, after a week full of rejection and failed opportunities, I drove my powerchair along the seawall and ended up on the pier. Sitting there by the water, I wept hysterically. I felt like my soul was dying. I couldn't get out of the cage of people's preconceived ideas of my limitations.

I kept crying out to God for help. Finally, I realized I couldn't change society's prejudices. Rather, I needed to shift my own perspective. I needed to focus on the word of God and his promises to me. The prophet Isaiah said: "But those who hope in the Lord will renew their strength. They will soar on wings like eagles; they will run and not grow weary, they will walk and not be faint." (Isaiah 40:31 NIV) I can honestly say that the Lord is working in me, dissipating my resentment and blessing me with new opportunities that are more favourable to his will and glory.

Dear Father in Heaven,

Racial tension and societal prejudice are on the rise. People are losing patience, becoming less empathetic and tolerant. There is a lack of common courtesy. Negativity is dominating social media. It is so easy to immediately voice our critical opinions online without contemplating the impact this has on others. We are less willing to take time to listen and understand the issues. In some respects, it feels like society is going backward, losing the ability to empathize and be compassionate and to treat each person with dignity.

Lord, as your representatives of Christ's love, let us refrain from quick judgement that demeans others. Teach us to empower one another with respect and understanding, building communities with integrity and inclusion. May we treat people with the same dignity you have shown in your unconditional love and acceptance toward us, knowing that we are ALL treasured in your eyes.

Lord, continue to bless us with your compassionate perspective, and mold our mind-sets with your holy grace so we can combat the injustices in honourable ways.

Lord, thank you for teaching me that I am complete in you and with your strength I can soar.

Amen

God desires us all to be released from our inner cages, free from past hurts and sin, defined by his holiness.

No Fare Gates
with God

After graduating from high school, I moved from a small town in northern British Columbia to the Greater Vancouver area to pursue my post-secondary education. It was quite a change for a small-town girl. I grew up in a non-accessible environment where I had to adapt and even advocate for accessibility when necessary.

For example, the only high school in town had no ramp and the school board wanted me to take my education by correspondence. My family, with the support of my elementary school teachers, advocated for a ramp so I could attend high school. I still had to take French by correspondence as there was no elevator to the second floor and the teacher refused to move the class downstairs to the main floor. Although it was challenging at times, I'm grateful to this day that I have always been integrated into the school system.

When I started college in the city, I began to experience the true meaning of accessibility, especially in the realm of transportation. Getting to the college from my place on public transit involved catching a bus to the SeaBus with a 15-minute crossing to downtown, followed by a SkyTrain ride, then lastly another bus to school. A one-way trip took two hours and this happened a few times per week. Even though it was long, I was grateful I had the opportunity to get an education and that wheelchair-accessible transit was at least possible.

I often feel incredibly fortunate to have been born within the era of the accessibility revolution. In reflecting, I imagine how difficult transportation was for people before my time as there really were no public wheelchair accommodations.

As my primary source of transportation is public transit, I take the bus, SeaBus and SkyTrain to travel all over the Greater Vancouver area. Until recently, it was quite easy to hop on transit as I merely needed to show my fare ticket or transit pass to the transit staff. But this all changed when fare gates were installed at the entrances and exits of the SeaBus and SkyTrain stations and the implementation of the Compass Card system. Now, in order to pass through a gate, I need to wave my Compass Card over the red light that is on the right side of the gate. For some people with disabilities, it's an impossible task as they don't have the mobility or strength to complete the transaction. As a result, they are locked out until a transit employee or a willing passenger comes by to help scan their Compass Card for them. Although the transit authority continues to make modifications to ease the process, it is still an ongoing issue for many people with disabilities.

Fortunately, in my case, I have the motor skills to reach up and scan the pass to pay and activate the gate. However, sometimes it takes me two or three attempts. Once the gate is open, I need to speed my chair through before it closes, which is not always easy to do. There are times when my arm goes into a spasm and I need to wait until my arm and hand relax before I can drive my chair. I consider myself one of the fortunate ones, even though this is another hurdle to overcome. I'm blessed to have the physical and mental ability to work through these types of obstacles to get to my destination, always reminding myself to be grateful for the accessibility I'm privileged to have.

Every time we use public transit we need to pay. However, in terms of our relationship with the Lord, the fare is already paid. Once we accept Jesus as our savior, we acknowledge that he made the greatest sacrifice by dying for our sins. Jesus gave us the gift of salvation and he paid our fare in full. This is called grace. This is what's so attractive about God. No longer are there any hurdles or barriers to God—we have complete access. The gate of grace is activated and will never close.

"And God raised us up with Christ and seated us with him in the heavenly realms in Christ Jesus, in order that in the coming ages he might show the incomparable riches of his grace, expressed in his kindness to us in Christ Jesus. For it is by grace you have been saved, through faith—and this is not from yourselves, it is the gift of God—not by works, so that no one can boast."

EPHESIANS 2:6-9 (NIV)

Dear Father in Heaven,

Lord, thank you that the gate to your Holy Spirit always remains open. We as human beings, especially as adults, often make things more complicated, or fail to believe in the simplicity of unconditional love.

The fact is, your love doesn't discriminate. Your grace and mercy have no bounds. You are dead set in removing any barriers that hinder the intimacy between us.

"We live restored to God and reconciled in the body of Christ. Through his crucifixion, hatred died. For *the Messiah has come to preach this sweet message of peace to you, the ones who were distant, and to those who are near. And now, because we are united to Christ, we both have equal and direct access in the realm of the Holy Spirit to come before the Father!"*

Ephesians 2:16-18 (TPT)

Life is full of adversity and struggle to overcome. However, it's the opposite with you Lord; you welcome us just as we are. We don't need to work for your love. It is so refreshing to have barrier-free access to you, Heavenly Father.

How blessed I am to have the peace and assurance of your unending nurture and love.

Amen

Imagine our Heavenly Father waiting for you. All you have to do is run and leap into his open arms.

The Value of Reliance

"*Yes, my soul, find rest in God; my hope comes from him. Truly he is my rock and my salvation; he is my fortress, I will not be shaken. My salvation and my honor depend on God; he is my mighty rock, my refuge. Trust in him at all times, you people; pour out your hearts to him, for God is our refuge.*"

Psalm 62:5-8 (NIV)

Occasionally I wish I could cook a meal, pour a cup of coffee or put lip balm on my lips when they're dry. There are times I would like to be less reliant on people, to have more flexibility and independence.

For the most part I'm not bothered by my dependence on others. This doesn't define my self-worth or my ability to be active in society. It's a reality that I have learned to accept and even embrace. Because of my experience of relying on care attendants to assist me, I have greater freedom and I'm able to accomplish more. Through this I have learned the value of reliance.

In Western society, there is a tendency to value independence as the main characteristic of strength and success. Asking for or needing help is typically a sign of weakness and can bring feelings of shame. Sometimes it's necessary to break down the walls of pride and the illusion of strength in order to gain the kind of independence that will lead to greater joy and accomplishments, especially with the Holy Spirit.

Throughout my adulthood I have chosen to make life decisions that put me in places where I needed to have faith and rely on God.

One of the biggest leaps of faith for me was moving out of a group home and into an apartment to live on my own. This was the first time in my life that I was going to be in charge of hiring my own care attendants, as well as managing all the household responsibilities. At that time, I didn't know how it was going to work out, but I knew in my heart that God would provide everything and that he would turn the impossible into the possible. Nearly twenty years later, he is still providing.

We are all dependent on God, yet paradoxically, we still find ourselves yearning for independence and relying on our own strength. May we consciously and purposefully relinquish some of our independence, yielding to the Holy Spirit, allowing God to nourish our souls with the food that only he can provide.

"Stunned and bewildered, his disciples asked, 'Then who in the world can possibly be saved?' Looking straight into their eyes, Jesus replied, 'Humanly speaking, no one, because no one can save himself. But what seems impossible to you is never impossible to God!'"

MATTHEW 19:25-26 (TPT)

Dear Father in Heaven,

Lord, I hunger for change and for your Holy Spirit to be revealed in a deeper way to all mankind.

Sometimes I'm astounded by how oblivious humanity can be. Are we so blind or too stubborn to see how empowering your Spirit is in our lives? Is it a power struggle? Is it our natural desire to be independent and self-reliant? Is it the greed for human comfort? Or is it the fear of letting go and putting our assurance in faith?

I'm mystified that our desire to be more intimate with you exists and yet we keep you at arm's length, contained in a box that we open periodically.

Able Soul

God, thank you for allowing me to experience your unconditional grace. There have been so many times when you came to my rescue, opened the doors and answered my heart's desire.

As a person living with a disability, I have learned to depend on you for the smallest things, to accept my circumstances and allow you to help me thrive beyond my ability. I wish that more people could see how magnificent you are in everyday life—how you care about the smallest details.

Your love is immaculate; your Spirit gives delicate radiance to life. This is reflected in your Son's story. It is the cornerstone of our holy heritage and of the legacy that we pass on.

I pray that as we fully embrace your Spirit we will become less prideful in human strength and relish more the awesomeness of your Spirit.

Amen

Dependence on God is like floating on water. Allow yourself to relax, surrender and trust. Feel the warmth of the Holy Spirit carrying you.

God is Faithful in Prayer

When I moved from a group home to live independently in an apartment, one of the things I prayed for was the opportunity to be of service. A drawback of having CP is that people tend to underestimate my abilities, especially with acts of service. Often when I offer to help they politely decline, not because they don't need help, but because they think it might be too hard for me.

"*The* LORD *is good to those whose hope is in him, to the one who seeks him; it is good to wait quietly for the salvation of the Lord.*"

LAMENTATIONS 3:25-26 (NIV)

Over the years I have learned to rely on God in this area. I have asked God to put me in places or situations where I can bring joy or lend a helping hand. It is a prayer I remember every so often. I trust God knows my heart's desire and will eventually fulfill that desire.

A remarkable answer to this prayer happened when I had a chance encounter with the daughter of my 94-year-old neighbour Blanche. She told me Blanche had fallen and was in the hospital recovering. I asked if I could visit and she replied that her mother would love that.

A couple of days later I went to visit. While I cruised up to the hospital in my power chair, I wondered if she would recognize me. I didn't know how disoriented she would be. It didn't really matter if she remembered me because I adored her so. Blanche is one of the sweetest, most joyful and positive people I know. Whenever I would run into her in the hallway or outside the apartment complex, she always lifted my day. Her joyful nature was contagious—the kind I aspire to have. What made her even more impressive was that she was legally blind and still lived on her own at her advanced age.

I arrived at the hospital and asked the nurse what room Blanche was in. God is so good. Not only did the nurse reply, but she led me to Blanche's bedside and announced to her that a friend had come to visit.

At first Blanche didn't recognize my voice because of my speech impediment, but she was persistent in finding out who I was. I kept repeating my name, but she still didn't understand. Finally, I spelled it. "L-u-c-y,"

I said, hoping she would figure it out. She did and was so gleeful and excited that I had come. We had an enjoyable conversation and she told me all about her fall. She also took much delight in a small gift that I had brought with me. Before I left I promised her I would return. As always, she told me to be careful while I was going home, saying, "Don't be dumb like me and fall."

On the way home, tears of joy and appreciation ran down my face as I reminisced on our visit and recalled the prayer I had prayed long ago. With a grateful heart, I proclaimed to God, "You are a remarkable Heavenly Father."

He never forgets the simple, seemingly unimportant desires of our hearts. It may take months or even years for God to fulfill our hearts' desires but he does it in such a magnificent and poignant way that it's worth waiting for. Trust that God knows your heart and will eventually answer your call.

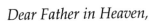

Dear Father in Heaven,

I'm honoured you know and remember my heart's desires. What an incredible fatherly gesture. You keep surprising me with opportunities that are in accordance with your will and legacy of love. Thank you for your confidence in my ability and that you don't discriminate against my frailties, but you see their beauty and turn my weaknesses into assets.

You are masterfully brilliant in how you orchestrate timing and events to answer our hearts' desires and how you not only bless us but others as well. Often, what we envision or how we would like you to answer our prayers is so minimal compared to your capability. I forget how limiting my imagination and perspective are.

Thank you, Lord, that we have the freedom to come to you with the simplicity of just disclosing our wishes and trusting you enough to leave them in your hands.

Amen

God does answer our heart's desires in sweet loving ways. Reminisce on your own answered prayers and blessings from the Lord, affirming his goodness.

Unclenching
My Hands

*O*ne of my favourite spiritual practices is Lent. It's a season to remember our holy heritage (the story of Jesus and his sacrifice)—to evaluate our spiritual well-being and be more intimate with God. In carrying on from my church upbringing, every year I try to come up with a practice or activity that will awaken my consciousness and remind me to be mindful of the Holy Spirit. Some years I would abstain from an activity like watching TV or fast one day a week. One year I decided to make the practice more physical and personal. During my prayer time I made an effort to turn my palms right side up and unclench my hands. I did this daily to demonstrate to God that I was present and available, centred on him and open to his will.

To the average person this might be a simple task that probably takes little thought and minimal concentration. In my case, since I have CP, I actually need to concentrate to get my hands palm side up and then wait for my fingers to unbend. This task might take a few tries but eventually my brain sends the message to the right body parts.

Unclenching my hands during Lent had a profound effect on me. I felt vulnerable and somewhat exposed in my body movements. It was uncomfortable in the moment but it was also strangely freeing. In a way I was letting go of my desire to be in control, acknowledging my dependence on God, while being present and more of a partner.

The second profound revelation for me was how reserved my spirit had become. Living on a tight budget has made me frugal. I look for ways to save, find the cheapest price or wait for a sale. I'm in the mind-set of being cautious, deciding what I need and what can wait. From a financial perspective this is necessary and wise. However, through my Lenten practice I realized my mind-set of frugality had transcended into other areas of my life, especially my faith.

In the beginning I was distraught by this realization, but I was also appreciative of the awakening, and the opportunity to change and redirect my mind-set. Even though I still need to be cautious financially, my faith and love for God can be free and unrestricted.

I will continue to unclench my hands during Lent and even afterward, not expecting anything, but allowing God the opportunity to take my hands anytime he wishes.

"*And in a similar way, the Holy Spirit takes hold of us in our human frailty to empower us in our weakness. For example, at times we don't even know how to pray, or know the best things to ask for. But the Holy Spirit rises up within us to super-intercedes on our behalf, pleading to God with emotional sighs too deep for words. God, the searcher of the heart, knows fully our longings, yet he also understands the desires of the Spirit, because the Holy Spirit passionately pleads before God for us, his holy ones, in perfect harmony with God's plan and our destiny.*"

ROMANS 8: 26-27 (TPT)

Dear Father in Heaven,

Thank you for the practice of Lent, a tradition that I savour every year. For me it's like an escape from the daily grind of life—a time to be less self-absorbed and put your Holy Spirit in the driver's seat.

I thank you for accepting my small gestures during Lent and masterfully revealing your wisdom and insight in ways that are so impactful to my mind and heart.

May I keep reminding myself that you are my pilot in life and allow me to be as gracious as you are. Although the journey may be turbulent at times, you, oh Lord, take me to the required destination and we always arrive at the right time.

Amen

Embracing the Holy Spirit, what small gesture can you make today to remind yourself to be more intimate with the Lord?

The Art
of Wrestling

"And in a similar way, the Holy Spirit takes hold of us in our human frailty to empower us in our weakness. For example, at times we don't even know how to pray, or know the best things to ask for. But the Holy Spirit rises up within us to super-intercede on our behalf, pleading to God with emotional sighs too deep for words."

ROMANS 8:26 (TPT)

One of my favourite recreational activities is climbing—indoor wall climbing or outdoor rock climbing. I took an interest in the sport when I attended a workshop hosted by The Canadian Adaptive

Climbing Society. This is where I meet with Brent who is an avid climber and the Executive Director. His passion is to make climbing accessible so that anyone including myself who has a physical disability is able to climb.

Climbing is a challenge for anyone, requiring tremendous physical dexterity, problem solving and determination. For me, it's a wrestling game as I try to make my body cooperate with my mind. First you have to ensure your foot is stable on the toe-hold, then have a firm hand grip to pull yourself up. I usually have to make several attempts before my body is anchored in the correct position. I feel a sense of accomplishment with every step taken. I am one more foot closer to the top!

There is a battle of the mind, as any climber can attest. Sometimes you are grappling with insecurities while wrestling your body into position. You learn how to cast off these negative mind intruders and continue climbing.

With having CP, wrestling with my body movements is a big part of my daily life. Because I have a lot of involuntary movements it can take me a few attempts to complete a task. Similarly, when it comes to my prayer life and listening to the Holy Spirit, I often have to struggle to quiet my thoughts and allowing my mind to calm down and be still.

If I had a child, one of the pearls of wisdom I would pass down is the art of wrestling, not physically in terms of a sport, but spiritually—grappling with your thoughts and doubts. Just as it takes practice to be proficient at a sport, it also takes practice to be a skillful listener, discerning the voice of the Holy Spirit. I would remind my child that in the beginning, it's always difficult to learn a new skill. If we can't get it right the first time, we tend to think we are failing or not good enough. As we practice any skill we gain more confidence. I would tell my child that grappling with your thoughts and emotions is natural, that it's okay to keep seeking and pursuing the answer. Just as in prayer, as we learn how to listen and recognize the voice of the Holy Spirit we begin to feel more comfortable resting in his presence. When this happens, it is beautiful and peaceful.

"God, the searcher of the heart, knows fully our longings, yet he also understands the desires of the Spirit, because the Holy Spirit passionately pleads before God for us, his holy ones, in perfect harmony with God's plan and our destiny."

ROMANS 8:27 (TPT)

When you pray, God will always find a way to untie the knots in your mind and heart. Just keep believing in him.

Dear Father in Heaven,

My mind is going in a thousand directions. I can't seem to tame my wandering thoughts. My desire when seeking solace, is to wait patiently, and listen for your voice. I stand before you wanting to calm down, to be still in your presence.

May I not be entangled by distractions. While grappling with my thoughts, Lord, grant me the discipline to meditate on you. The act of calming my mind and body will eventually lead to a deeper connection with the Holy Spirit, and to the secret place where my soul can connect with yours.

Lord, as I quiet my mind, please fill me up with your gentle peace.

May I rest in the stillness of your presence knowing that you will refresh my mind and renew my soul.

Amen

Are you ready for a Holy massage? Close your eyes, relax and enjoy the healing touch of the Lord.

Hunger to Serve

Some of the most profound experiences in my life resulted from acts of service and being able to assist others. One element that we sometimes fail to acknowledge is the importance of enabling others to serve. Having the opportunity to serve is so empowering and embodies the goodness of the human spirit. As a person living with a disability, I'm more sensitive to this human need, and deeply appreciate whenever I'm given the opportunity to serve.

"You, my brothers and sisters, were called to be free. But do not use your freedom to indulge the flesh; rather, serve one another humbly in love. For the entire law is fulfilled in keeping this one command: 'Love your neighbor as yourself."

GALATIANS 5:13-14 (NIV)

Able Soul

Whenever I offer to help, more times than not, my offer is politely declined. Sometimes I feel people prejudge me and assume it might be too much for me to handle or that I'm not capable of doing the task at all. Of course, sometimes my offers are declined solely because the person doesn't want or require help. As a lifelong recipient of kindness, I'm conscious of the courage it takes to offer assistance. My rule of thumb is to accept generosity whenever possible. This, in itself, is a way of serving and empowering others—a way of affirming their spirits.

There are times when I have an unquenchable desire to serve that my spirit feels like it's stuck in a cage. At such times, I imagine how God must feel as he experiences rejection on a daily basis, hour by hour. All he longs for is that we be receptive to his love, anointing and divine healing. By being more receptive to this desire in others, we learn to be more receptive to the Lord.

One of my favourite experiences of being able to serve happened at a women's prayer retreat. During the last session there was the option of washing one another's feet. I was overcome with the desire to participate in this sacred ritual. The atmosphere was solemn and prayerful. I tried as quietly as possible to squirm down from my wheelchair onto the floor and crawled to the bowl of water. I dove my hand into the bowl, indicating to my friend I was ready to wash her feet. Unbeknownst to me, everyone in the room was touched by the Holy Spirit because of this gesture.

That moment was profound. I felt my spirit being released from my inner cage as God orchestrated the setting where I could be free to serve. I genuinely felt like my Heavenly Father's daughter, a true disciple of Jesus, empowered and affirmed by the Holy Spirit.

God sets the atmosphere for people to be open to receiving a divine blessing. This is why we are on earth. We often focus on how we can serve and how we can love and support our community. But sometimes the most helpful way is by empowering others, allowing the Holy Spirit to minister to us through them.

Dear Father in Heaven,

How we long to be more like-minded with your Son, to follow in the steps of Jesus with his great servant's heart. He had the ability and foresight to look beyond the perceived circumstances and see into people's hearts.

Jesus didn't always take the routine course of serving others, but waited until he gained insight as to what was really required and what would be most beneficial to the person. When led by the Holy Spirit, he would allow others to serve him as a means of empowerment and redemption.

Sometimes we get caught up in our own ways and do more harm than good. May we all learn to live like Jesus, seeing others through your eyes and serving them in ways that you call us to.

Fill me with your wisdom and insight, so that I will become your radiant light and give hope to my neighbours, especially the brokenhearted.

Amen

It is an honour to serve and to be a true disciple following in the steps of Jesus! Let's not take this for granted. How can you embody Jesus' way of empowering others to serve?

Guarding the Sacred

I have a website with my blog called *Able Soul*. My blog is sacred to me as it contains most of my reflective writing pieces, which are very personal and will hopefully inspire others on their faith journey.

My website has been hacked a couple of times. The files were contaminated with malicious content. Although the web host repaired the contaminated files, I lost confidence in their ability to protect and secure my website after the second hack.

A web host is the gatekeeper that maintains all of your website's files, supposedly backing up the domain and providing security measures to protect your website from hackers and spammers. Since this is beyond my technical scope, I decided to find another gatekeeper that was more user-friendly and would take the extra security measures to safeguard my blog.

Of course, the responsibility of protecting my website is not completely up to the web host. It is also mine as the owner, to take additional security precautions such as downloading anti-spam software and other security plug-ins that will help monitor and safeguard my website.

As parents or guardians, we take security measures and set boundaries to protect the welfare of our children. For valuables, such as jewellery, stocks, bonds, wills and sacred personal items, they are often stored in a safety-deposit box. However, sometimes we neglect to safeguard what is most sacred and intangible—our personal relationship with God—which is crucial in sustaining our souls.

"Wisdom is a gift from a generous God, and every word he speaks is full of revelation and becomes a fountain of understanding within you. For the Lord has a hidden storehouse of wisdom made accessible to his godly lovers. He becomes your personal bodyguard as you follow his ways, protecting and guarding you as you choose what is right."
Proverbs 2:6-8 (TPT)

The Book of Proverbs is all about preventing "malicious content" and safeguarding our personal relationship with the Lord as we love and serve him.

Not only does Proverbs outline measures for us to protect our hearts, but it also counsels us against becoming hackers ourselves, instructing us how to treat others in a godly manner.

As with the process of securing a website, we are also given knowledge and wisdom to take the precautions to guard what is most sacred, thus allowing our intimacy with God to remain steadfast and ultimately protect our souls.

Dear Father in Heaven,

I admit sometimes I do neglect our relationship, not spending enough time in your presence or taking time to converse and listen to you. However, the thing I'm most ashamed of is my lack of knowledge about your Holy Word.

To be honest, I really suck at reading the Bible. I often get discouraged that I can't retain the information or that I should know more about the context and passages. What is more idiotic is that I allow my disgrace to get the best of me and discourage me from delving into your Word. It's a cycle I need to break.

I hunger for knowledge and wisdom as they are the foundation to growing in spiritual maturity.

Able Soul

Lord, my love and adoration for you is so sacred I want to do everything to honour and protect what I have with you — to be a true disciple. You protect my well-being in so many ways. I want to get rid of any hackers, so, Lord, please show me areas in my life that are preventing me from drawing close to you and not safeguarding our intimacy.

Amen

 The Lord is our holy bodyguard. Wisdom is the best defense mechanism to ward off the hackers in your life.

A Faith-Filled Adventure

"*Now faith brings our hopes into reality and becomes the foundation needed to acquire the things we long for. It is all the evidence required to prove what is still unseen. This testimony of faith is what previous generations were commended for. Faith empowers us to see that the universe was created and beautifully coordinated by the power of God's words! He spoke and the invisible realm gave birth to all that is seen.*"

HEBREWS 11:1-3 (TPT)

W hen I reached my fourth decade of life on earth, I chose to celebrate in a special way that honoured the Lord. With that goal in mind, I took a leap of faith, affirming to God that I trusted him wholeheartedly with my life's aspirations. Craving a small adventure, I decided to go on a short excursion.

My plan was to escape city life for a weekend getaway to a little town called Gibsons, on the Sunshine Coast, across the inlet from Vancouver. To get there from my place requires two lengthy bus rides with a 40-minute ferry ride in between.

For any kind of overnight travel, I require personal care assistance as well as wheelchair-accessible accommodations. I researched lodgings online and called around to find a room with a wheelchair-accessible bathroom. This is key in determining where I can stay.

To use the washroom, I require a grab bar on the wall beside the toilet so I can hold on and transfer myself from the power chair. After numerous inquiries, I breathed a sigh of relief when, finally, the hotel booking agent was able to meet my request and confirmed the washroom was fully wheelchair accessible.

I also require assistance with dressing and preparing my breakfast in the morning, so I made arrangements with a former care attendant who had moved to the Sunshine Coast. The morning before I left, to my dismay, I received an email informing me that she was sick and was unable to assist me. Not to be deterred, I called a friend who has family living on the Sunshine Coast to see if he knew anyone who could help me. He told me he would try to find someone.

In order to catch the ferry on time, I left the city with a feeling of uneasiness, unaware if I had an alternate care assistant. However, I still had confidence my accommodations were secure. I had faith the rest would fall into place.

When I arrived at the hotel, I immediately motored into my suite to investigate the bathroom. My heart sank—the grab bar was in the wrong place! It was not adjacent to the toilet, which I specified, but located on the opposite wall. And at quite a distance! Anyone using the grab bar would have to be at least seven feet tall with exceptionally long legs and arms! That ain't me.

I remained calm, trying not to panic. Quickly thinking of alternative options, hoping there was an open coffee shop or restaurant nearby with a universally accessible wheelchair bathroom, I set off on my quest. Gibsons is a relatively small town with one main street. As I strolled around, I kept looking for a viable washroom. I ended up in a women's clothing store and asked the clerk where there was a wheelchair-accessible bathroom. To my delight, she said I could use the one in her store, but it didn't have a grab bar. My heart sank farther. By now, my bladder was about to explode!

There was another female customer in the store who overheard my predicament. She kindly offered to help me in the washroom. The owner also volunteered to assist. I asked if they were comfortable helping me and they replied, "We are all women." Clearly it wasn't an issue. I knew in my heart this was divinely orchestrated by God and felt comfortable with them assisting me.

With respect to the care attendant situation, God also answered my prayers!

The friend who I'd called before I left, asked his cousin if she could assist me. Not available for the entire time, she and another friend of hers (both of whom were nurses) took turns helping me throughout my weekend adventure. Even though they both had weekend shifts, they were so kind and graciously managed to lend a helping hand at the last minute. They were both angels!

What a wonderful start to my fourth decade: experiencing an incredible adventure of faith! This was such a testament to God's provision, in his fatherly ways, when I truly trusted him. The blessing of trusting God, of having faith in him, has granted me opportunities that would seem impossible if I had depended solely on my own strength and understanding. What a gift to treasure!

Dear Father in Heaven,

Thank you for the comfort of knowing you are the great provider. It is so easy to lose sight of this. How frustrating it is for you, Lord, that we continually doubt, wondering if you really will come to our rescue. May we not forget how wonderful you are and always trust your love for us will never change or cease.

I'm grateful to be secure in knowing you are my ultimate caretaker. Even though I may waver, I will always reaffirm my faith in you, remembering your diligence in answering my prayers.

> *"By entering through faith into what God has always wanted to do for us—set us right with him … We throw open our doors to God and discover at the same moment that he has already thrown open his door to us. We find ourselves standing where we always hoped we might stand—out in the wide open spaces of God's grace and glory, standing tall and shouting our praise … we're never left feeling shortchanged. Quite the contrary—we can't round up enough containers to hold everything God generously pours into our lives through the Holy Spirit!"*
>
> Romans 5:1a, 2 & 5 (MSG)

To you, Oh Lord, all glory and honour is given.

Amen

Afterword

*M*y Dear Reader,

This book has taken me on an unexpected journey of discovering my voice. I felt called by God to write this book, oblivious to what this undertaking would entail, but learning to trust his voice within me. In the beginning I was petrified as I didn't believe in my ability to write.

Overcoming my lack of confidence meant I needed to relinquish past hurts of having my speaking voice completely ignored or not fully listened to. Unfortunately, this can be a reality of having a speech impediment. In this fast-paced society we are so rushed that often we don't take the time to truly listen, respect and value each other's differences. Not only did I have to forgive, I had to surrender my insecurities to God and trust him to lead the way. Because of this I have a deep appreciation for you taking the time to read my book.

People like myself require extra time to be heard, in fact, so does God. I was reminded of this as I was writing, praying for wisdom and guidance, waiting for the Spirit to reveal what was needed.

Initially I began my journey by sharing thoughts on my blog. With positive comments from readers and by God's grace, my confidence slowly increased. I uncovered the gift of my writing voice. I still go through periods of writer's block but I'm learning to press on and lean into God's goodness and wisdom.

Finishing this book has taken a lot longer than I anticipated but I've gained a new kind of freedom. Finding my voice and testifying to God's goodness are invaluable gifts.

May you be blessed in delightful ways. I pray these reflections and prayers will serve as a catalyst, reinvigorating you with a hunger to be more intimate with God. I hope they take you on a soulful adventure with him and awaken you to the possibilities of your Able Soul.

Come join me in creating a place where we can share our God stories, uplift the Lord and encourage one another. I'd love to have you share *your* Able Soul story on:

- my website: http://ablesoul.ca
- facebook: https://www.facebook.com/ablesoul.ca
- instagram: https://www.instagram.com/ablesoul

Peace and joy to you,
Lucy